Captain Bligh in Wapping
1785–1790

Madge Darby

Second revised edition

Published by The History of Wapping Trust – Charity Reg. No. 290087
Design © The History of Wapping Trust 2017
Text © Madge Darby 2017

ISBN 978–1–873086–07–0

Acknowledgements:

Original Text   -   Madge Darby

Design and Layout   -   John Tarby FRPS

Additional Research   -   Ray Newton

Proofreading   -   Helen Keep

Printing   -   Aldgate Press

Picture credits:

History of Wapping Trust

Tower Hamlets Local History Library & Archives

Museum in Docklands

Museum of London PLA Collection

London Metropolitan Archives

John Tarby collection

Ray Newton collection

Captain Cook Memorial Museum

Tate Britain

National Maritime Museum, Greenwich and Cornwall

William Foreman/University of Michigan

With thanks to:
Waitrose St Katharine Docks, St George PLC and Betzy Dinesen

Outside Cover - "A Dockyard at Wapping" by Francis Holman c.1780-84
Inside Cover - Composite map of Wapping and Shadwell from four sections of Richard Horwood's Street Plan of London 1799, compiled by John Tarby

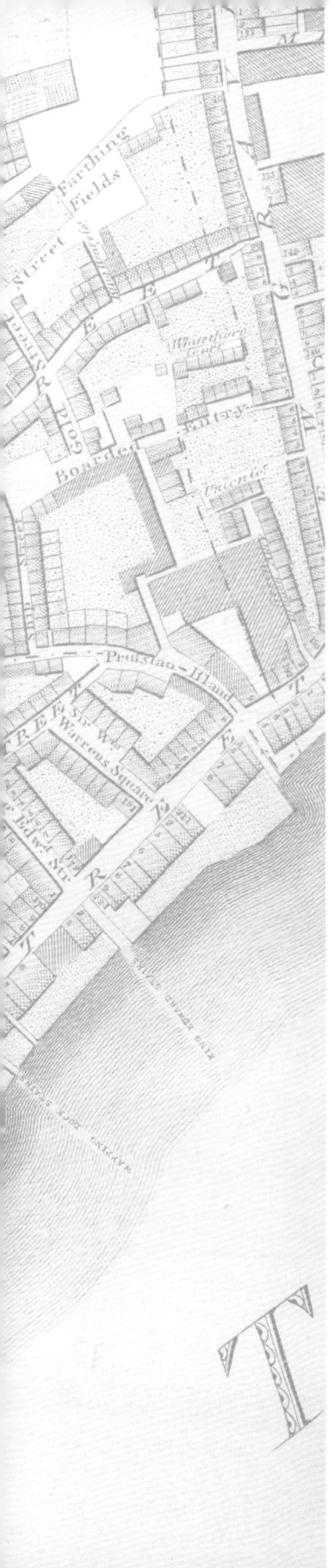

CONTENTS

Foreword

			page
1	William Bligh	1754–86	9
2	The Breadfruit Scheme	1787	19
3	HM Armed Vessel *Bounty*	1787–88	23
4	Tahiti	1788	27
5	Mutiny	1789	33
6	Voyage Home	1789–90	39
7	Breadfruit Success	1791–1800s	47
8	Additional Information		57

William Bligh by John Russell RA, 1791. Official portrait made for the Admiralty

Foreword

As a great-great-great-grandson of Vice-Admiral William Bligh RN, FRS (1754–1817) and also a long-term friend of Madge Darby, I'm delighted that the History of Wapping Trust has published a second revised edition of *Captain Bligh in Wapping* to acknowledge the 200th anniversary of my ancestor's death.

Bligh has been much maligned over the decades since the events aboard His Majesty's Armed Vessel *Bounty* were turned into a legend by novelists and movie-makers. Yet, in reality, he was a national hero who saved the lives of all but one man (killed by natives on Tofua) of the 19 squeezed into an open boat that was cast adrift in the open ocean, at a spot over 4,000 miles away from the then nearest known outpost of civilisation. It was an epic journey that remains one of the greatest maritime achievements of all time.

The book describes William's connection with, and his home in, Wapping, near to the River Thames, in the 1780s. It's a fascinating 'before the *Bounty*' insight into when he was a happily married family man and a young sea captain of ships sailing to and from the West Indies islands.

Thank you to the History of Wapping Trust for writing and publishing this account.

Maurice Bligh

Maurice Bligh is descended from William Bligh's third daughter, Elizabeth, who was born in Wapping in 1786. She married her second cousin, Richard Bligh, a lawyer, in 1817.

Captain Bligh in Wapping 1785–1790

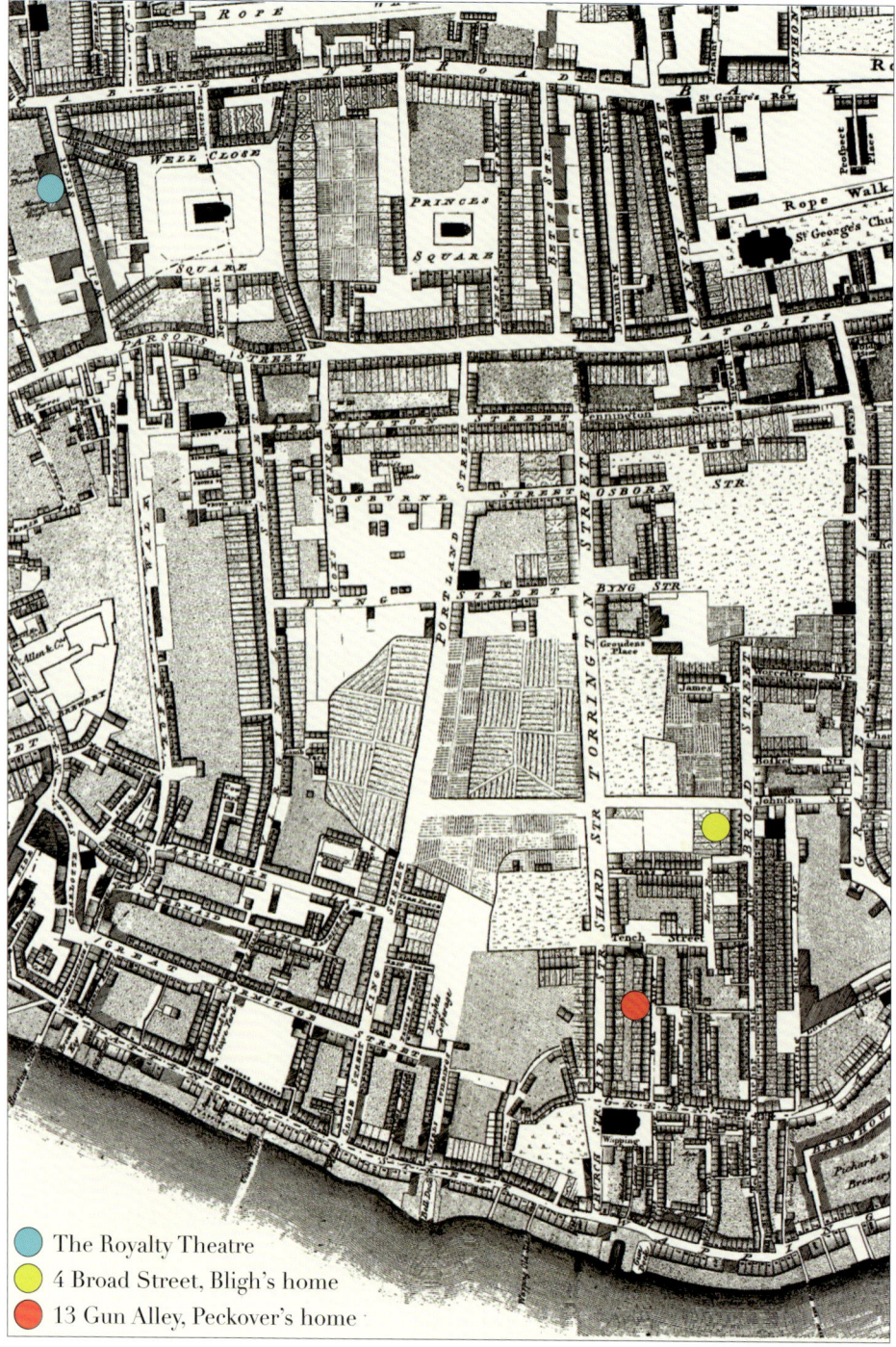

○ The Royalty Theatre
○ 4 Broad Street, Bligh's home
○ 13 Gun Alley, Peckover's home

Sheet from Richard Horwood's Plan of London (1799), showing the location of Bligh's house, Peckover's house and the Royalty Theatre

1 - William Bligh

Research by the History of Wapping Trust has revealed that Captain Bligh was living in Wapping when he set sail on his voyage in the *Bounty*. This voyage led to the famous mutiny in 1789, though in fact it was a piratical seizure rather than a typical 18th-century naval mutiny.

Until now, research into Bligh's private life has concentrated on his early life in Plymouth, Devon and his later life in Lambeth, south London, and Farningham Manor, Kent. The crucial period leading to his voyage in the *Bounty* has been neglected.

William Bligh was born on 9th September 1754, the son of Francis and Jane Bligh and of a distinguished Cornish family who held the Manor of Tinten in St Tudy, and who were also related to the Earls of Darnley. As was usual, younger sons went into the professions or services and Bligh's father, a fifth son, held a sinecure in the customs service in Plymouth.

Left St Andrew's church, Plymouth, was destroyed in the Blitz but the bell tower survived.
Centre The original octagonal font in which Bligh was baptised. It had been swapped for a Gothic Revival design by the Victorians so was not lost during the Blitz. The font was re-discovered after WW2 in a local garden and returned to the church when that was rebuilt.
Right Sculpture of Zachary Mudge (1694–1769), Prebendary of Exeter, Vicar of St Andrew's, Plymouth. Photos by John Tarby, 2017.

William was baptised by the Reverend Zachary Mudge in St Andrew's church (now the Minster Church of St Andrew), Plymouth on 4th October 1754.

Captain Bligh in Wapping 1785–1790

Bligh first appeared on a ship's books in 1762 when he was seven years old. He was entered as a "Captain's Servant" in HM Ship *Monmouth*. This gave rise to the belief that he started as a cabin boy but in the 18th century boys were supposed to serve two years at sea before becoming midshipmen in the Royal Navy. Captains were allowed more servants than they needed, so they used the spare places to enter their sons (as Captain Cook did), or the sons of their friends, on the books to help them get their time in. The boys did not even join the ships but usually remained at school. Bligh was probably entered at the request of the ship's surgeon, John Bond, who was married to Bligh's older half sister, Catherine.

William Bligh by John Webber RA, 1776

In fact, Bligh went to sea in 1770 when he signed on as an able seaman in HMS *Hunter*. This gave rise to a further misconception that Bligh was a common seaman but aspiring naval officers had to serve six years at sea before they could take the oral examination that qualified them to be commissioned as lieutenants. As there were not enough midshipmen's berths available, they signed on as able seamen and were promoted to acting midshipmen by the captain.

Bligh became an official midshipman six months later when a berth became available. He was then 16.

He took his lieutenant's examination in 1776 when he was 21. He passed but could not find a post immediately as a lieutenant.

1 - William Bligh

Bligh was offered the post of master in HM Ship *Resolution* on Captain Cook's third and final Pacific voyage. The master was the officer responsible for navigation. The post later developed into that of navigating officer with commissioned rank but at that time was held by a warrant officer. Cook was by then (1776) the most famous navigator in the world and there was great competition for any post on the voyage. Bligh was glad to accept the offer, which meant that he was practising navigation directly under Cook's command.

The voyage was a disastrous one as Cook was killed in 1779 by the natives in Hawaii. The *Resolution* was accompanied by another ship, HMS *Discovery*, and her captain, Charles Clerke, transferred to the *Resolution* and took command of the expedition but he died a few months later, leaving the two ships without either of the captains they had set out with.

James Cook by John Webber RA, c.1782

This left Bligh with more responsibility than ever for navigation and the ships returned safely to London in 1780.

Bligh was commissioned as a lieutenant in 1781, when he was 26. In the same year he married Elizabeth Betham in the Isle of Man. She was slightly older than he, 27.

Captain Bligh in Wapping 1785–1790

Elizabeth was reputed to be a beauty and, according to Bligh, had an:

extreme horror of the sea, the sound of gun or thunder.

The marriage was, nevertheless, a very happy one. Bligh wrote to his wife:

I love you dearer than ever a woman was loved.

The end of the American War of Independence led to Bligh being put on half-pay in 1783 but Mrs Bligh's uncle, Duncan Campbell, was a wealthy shipowner and gave him command of a series of merchant ships.

Elizabeth Bligh by John Russell RA, 1802

It was during this period that Bligh and his wife came to live in Wapping. They arrived in 1785 and by then they had two daughters, Harriet, who was four, and Mary who was one. The family was quite affluent as pay was much better in the merchant service than in the Royal Navy. Bligh was earning about £500 pa, a high income in those days (about £100,000 in 2017).

Eighteenth-century Wapping was an interesting place. Dr Johnson advised Boswell to "explore

1 - William Bligh

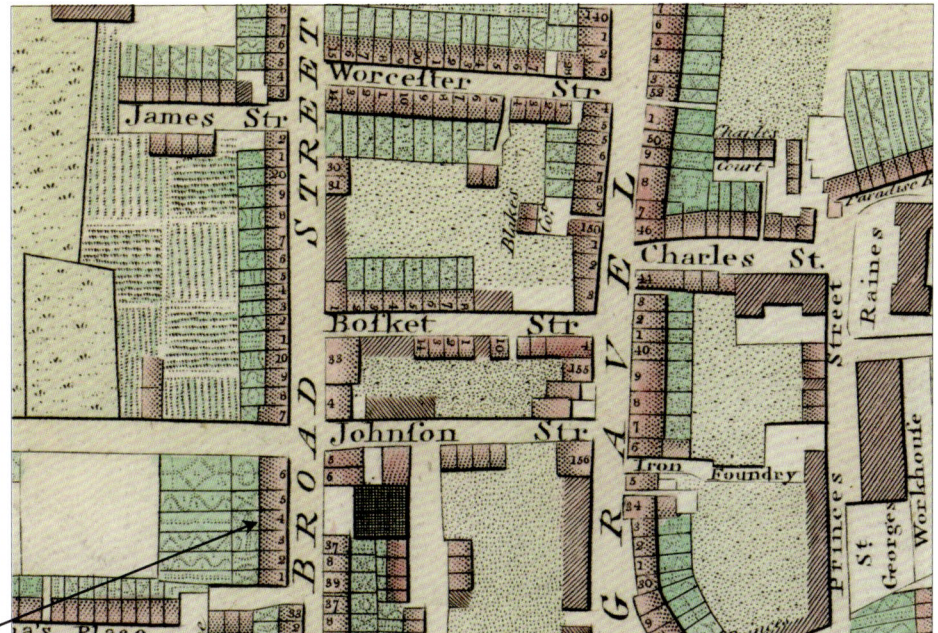

Detail from Richard Horwood's Plan of London (1799), showing the location of 4 Broad Street, Wapping – Bligh's house

Photo of Red Lion Street by HT Melby, 1899. Looking from Green Bank north up the former Anchor and Hope Alley towards the former Broad Street with St George-in-the-East in the distance

Captain Bligh in Wapping 1785–1790

Wapping". It was the birthplace of John Newton, who wrote the words of the hymn *Amazing Grace*, and of Hannah Lightfoot, who was, improbably, supposed to have been secretly married to King George III. Wapping was also the home of Hannah Snell, who disguised herself as a man and joined the marines. There were 36 taverns by the River Thames and pirates were still hanged at Execution Dock. It was a varied community, including seafarers of all ranks – from black seamen to naval officers. Captain Cook had lived in nearby Shadwell as a young man.

The Bligh family lived in Broad Street, a new wide street built in the 18th century, leading out of the older, narrower Anchor and Hope Alley. Bligh's house was probably similar to the Georgian houses in Red Lion Street which survived until the 1930s, when they were demolished by the London County Council, having fallen into disrepair as a result of the poverty and overcrowding brought by the docks.

22 Red Lion Street, Wapping, 1928

Broad Street was in the parish of St George-in-the-East and the Bligh

Broad Street
The names of Anchor and Hope Alley and Broad Street were abolished in 1891 when they were merged into the existing Red Lion Street. In 1939, Red Lion Street was renamed Reardon Street by the London County Council.

family attended St George's. The rector, Dr Herbert Mayo, was famous for his work among the black seamen. One of his curates wrote:

> *I suppose no clergyman in England ever baptised so many black men... The attachment of these poor people to him was very great.*

On 24th March 1786, Mrs Bligh gave birth to a third daughter, Elizabeth, who was baptised in St George's on 5th May.

St George-in-the-East. Photo by John Tarby, 2017

Captain Bligh in Wapping 1785-1790

While he was living in Wapping, Bligh was given command of the *Britannia*, one of Campbell's merchant ships, and was approached by Fletcher Christian, who applied for a place in the ship. Christian had been a midshipman in the Royal Navy but was also ashore as a result of the outbreak of peace.

According to Fletcher Christian's brother, Edward, a lawyer who later undertook his defence, Bligh:

> *returned a polite answer, that he was sorry he could not take Christian, having then his complement of officers.*

Christian persisted, saying:

> *if Captain Bligh would permit him to mess with the gentlemen, he would readily enter his ship as a Foremast-man until there was a vacancy among the officers.*

Bligh agreed, and Edward Christian said his brother:

> *spoke of Captain Bligh with great respect: he said, that... the Captain had been kind to him in shewing him the use of his charts and instruments; but at the same time he observed, that Captain Bligh was very passionate; yet he seemed to pride himself in knowing how to humour him.*

Christian made a bad impression on the first mate, Edward Lamb, who later wrote to Bligh:

> *I saw your partiality for the young man... though he went about every point of duty with a degree of indifference, that to me was truly unpleasant, but you were blind to his faults.*

Bligh and Fletcher Christian became friends and Christian visited Bligh's home and played with his children.

1 - William Bligh

*Contemporary impression of a young
Fletcher Christian before the mutiny,
by John Lockett.
Used as a commemorative medal at the
2014 Commonwealth Games*

Captain Bligh in Wapping 1785–1790

A breadfruit tree and its fruit (inset) at the Eden Project, Cornwall. Photos by John Tarby, 2002

Breadfruit

Artocarpus altilis is a species of flowering tree in the mulberry and jackfruit family (*Moraceae*), originating in the South Pacific and eventually spreading to the rest of Oceania. British and French navigators introduced a few Polynesian seedless varieties to the Caribbean islands during the late 18th century and today it is grown in some 90 countries throughout South and Southeast Asia, the Pacific, the Caribbean, Central America and Africa. The name breadfruit is derived from the texture of the moderately ripe fruit when cooked, similar to freshly baked bread and having a potato-like flavour.

2 - The Breadfruit Scheme

While Bligh was living in Wapping, a scheme was proposed to transplant the breadfruit tree from Tahiti in the South Pacific to the West Indies.

The breadfruit project has been criticised on the grounds that the breadfruit was intended as cheap food for slaves, but, in promoting it, the Society of Arts said:

> *mankind in general would be gainers by it.*

This certainly included the negro slaves of the West Indies, who were mostly like serfs under the feudal system. They were given a small piece of land that they had to cultivate to feed themselves and their families, as well as working on their owner's plantation.

Women selling plantains at a street market in Cameroon, Central Africa. Photo by William Foreman, 2013

Food that was cheap and needed little labour was, therefore, likely to be of great benefit to them. The slaves and other subsistence

Captain Bligh in Wapping 1785–1790

farmers lived mostly on plantains, or cooking bananas, and they all suffered great hardship when there was a bad harvest or the plantains were devastated by hurricanes.

It was hoped that the breadfruit would provide an alternative crop to mitigate these famines, especially as the breadfruit tree was better able to withstand hurricanes than the plantain.

*Sir Joseph Banks
by Sir Joshua Reynolds RA, 1773*

The principal promoter of the scheme was Sir Joseph Banks, the British naturalist, explorer and botanist and President of the Royal Society of London, who had seen the breadfruit when he had sailed with Cook on his first Pacific voyage in HM Bark *Endeavour*.

The Navy Board surveyed several ships to see whether they would be suitable for the breadfruit voyage, including the *William Pitt*, which lay off King Edward Stairs in Wapping Wall. She was not considered strong enough but another ship, the collier *Bethia*, a vessel of 215 tons, moored off Wapping Old Stairs, seemed more promising.

Gun Dock near Wapping Old Stairs by Thomas Hosmer Shepherd, 1850. The bell tower of St John of Wapping is in the background

2 - The Breadfruit Scheme

On 21st May 1787, Sir Joseph Banks visited Wapping Old Stairs to inspect the *Bethia*. With him were Mr Mitchell, an officer of the Navy Board, and David Nelson, a botanist who had sailed with Cook and Bligh in the *Resolution* and who was to go with the expedition to collect and take care of the breadfruit.

They decided the *Bethia* would be suitable for transporting the breadfruit plants. She was purchased by the Navy Board for £1,950 (about £400,000 in 2017) and renamed HM Armed Vessel *Bounty*.

Miseries of London – Wapping Old Stairs by Thomas Rowlandson, 1807

Wapping Old Stairs and causeway at low tide. Photo by John Tarby, 2014

Captain Bligh in Wapping 1785–1790

Bligh was appointed to command the *Bounty* and wrote to Banks:

4 Broad Street, St George's East

August 6/1787.

Sir,

I arrived yesterday from Jamaica and should have instantly paid my respects to you had not Mr Campbell told me you were not to return from the country until Thursday. I have heard the flattering news of your great goodness to me, intending to honor me with the command of the vessel which you propose to go to the South Seas, for which, after offering you my most grateful thanks, I can only assure you I shall endeavour, and I hope succeed, in deserving such a trust. I await your commands, and am, with the sincerest respect,

yours, etc.

Wm. Bligh.

3 - HM Armed Vessel Bounty

MGM's replica of the Bounty built in 1960 for its feature film, "Mutiny on the Bounty". Photo by Dan Askberger, 2010

Bligh remained a lieutenant in rank when he was given command of the *Bounty* and took a considerable cut in pay. As a lieutenant in the Royal Navy he was paid four shillings a day (about £40 in 2017). Bligh was entered in the muster book as lieutenant and commander (the equivalent of a modern-day lieutenant commander) but was, of course, described and addressed as Captain Bligh.

He took Fletcher Christian with him as a master's mate, a senior midshipman. He also took, as gunner, William Peckover, who had sailed with Cook on all three of his voyages of discovery and was gunner of the *Discovery* on Cook's last voyage. Peckover lived in Wapping at No 13 Gun Alley which ran down towards the River Thames from Tench Street to Green Bank.

One of the *Bounty*'s midshipmen was Peter Heywood, who

HMAV *Bounty*
Bounty was originally known as *Bethia*, a collier built in 1784 at the Blaydes shipyard in Hull, Yorkshire.
The vessel was purchased by the Royal Navy for £1,950 on 23rd May 1787, refit and renamed His Majesty's Armed Vessel *Bounty*. The ship was relatively small at 215 tons but had three masts and was full-rigged. After conversion at Deptford for the breadfruit expedition, she was equipped with four 4-pounder (1.8 kg) cannons and ten swivel guns.

Captain Bligh in Wapping 1785-1790

was 15 and going to sea for the first time. Heywood came from the Isle of Man and stayed with Bligh and his wife in Wapping before the voyage.

Bligh also took his servant, John Smith, who lived with him when ashore, and probably lived in his house in Wapping.

The *Bounty* sailed from Spithead on 23rd December 1787.

Peckover had more responsibility than was usually given to a gunner because, apart from Captain Bligh, the *Bounty* had no commissioned officers. When the crew was divided into three watches, the first was put in the charge of John Fryer, the Master, the second in Peckover's charge, and the third in the charge of Fletcher Christian.

Peckover was by then over 40 and suffered from rheumatism. On the outward voyage, Bligh recorded:

> *My Gunner has been laid up a few days with a Rheumatic Complaint, but is now doing duty again.*

Bligh kept on his house in Wapping and left his family there. Mrs Bligh was pregnant when he left on his voyage and on 11th May 1788 she gave birth to twin girls, Frances and Jane, who were baptised in St George's on 6th June.

A view of the Cape of Good Hope painted on board the "Resolution" by William Hodges RA, 1778

William Hodges
William Hodges RA (1744–97) was an English painter. He was a member of James Cook's second voyage to the Pacific Ocean and is best known for the sketches and paintings of locations he visited on that voyage, including Table Bay, Tahiti, Easter Island and the Antarctic.

3 - HM Armed Vessel Bounty

By then Bligh was at the Cape of Good Hope. On 2nd March he had recorded:

> *I gave to Mr Fletcher Christian, whom I had before directed to take charge of the third watch, a written order to act as lieutenant.*

Christian was thus promoted to be second in command.

Bligh was not, by the standards at the time, a harsh captain. On any objective criteria, such as the number of floggings or the punishment for individual offences, he was among the least severe of 18th-century sea captains. He wrote:

> *We are all in good spirits and my little ship fit to go round a half-score of worlds. My men all active good fellows, and what has given me much pleasure is that I have not yet been obliged to punish anyone... I am happy to hope I shall bring them all home well.*

Lawrence Lebogue, the *Bounty*'s sailmaker, said later:

> *Captain Bligh was not a person fond of flogging his men; and some of them deserved hanging, who had only a dozen.*

The chief accusation brought against Bligh by Edward Christian was that he was liable to outbursts of temper and that when anyone argued with him, or failed to carry out his orders, he assailed them with a tirade of swearing. Bligh did, however, suffer from migraines and most people agreed that he soon forgot his anger.

Lebogue said:

> *I have heard the Captain damn the people, like many other captains; but he was never angry with a man the next minute.*

Captain Bligh in Wapping 1785–1790

Midshipman John Hallett put it more delicately:

> *I will by no means affirm, that I never heard Captain Bligh express himself in warm or hasty language, when the conduct of his officers or people has displeased him; but every seafaring gentleman must be convinced, that situations frequently occur in a ship when the most mild officer will be driven, by the circumstances of the moment, to utter expressions which the strict standard of politeness will not warrant.*

"Poedua, the daughter of Orio" by John Webber RA, 1777

Poedua
John Webber RA first painted Poedua's portrait in 1777 during the three days when she, her husband and brother were hostages on board the ship *Discovery* as Cook pressured her father into returning two deserters. She was 15 at the time and pregnant. This is one of the earliest images of a Polynesian woman produced by a European painter.

John Webber
John Webber RA (1751–93) was an English artist who also served as the official artist on Captain James Cook's third voyage of discovery around the Pacific (1776–80) aboard HM Ship *Resolution*. Webber is best known for his images of Australasia, Hawaii and Alaska.

4 - Tahiti

"*HMS Resolution and HMS Adventure in Matavai Bay, Tahiti*" by William Hodges RA, 1776. Tahiti, previously also known as Otaheite, is the largest island in the Windward group of French Polynesia. The island is located in the archipelago of the Society Islands in the central southern Pacific Ocean

The *Bounty* arrived in Tahiti in October 1788 and the crew spent five months on the island Bligh described as:

> *the Paradise of the world.*

It must have seemed like paradise to the seamen, who led hard lives at sea and ashore. There was an abundance of food, obtained with little effort, and lovely women only too ready to receive their advances.

Bligh recorded:

> *To prevent as much as possible any thing which might occasion disputes, I desired Mr. Peckover, the Gunner, to undertake the management of our traffic with the natives.*

Captain Bligh in Wapping 1785–1790

This included both private transactions by the crew and the victualling of the ship, as Bligh explained:

> *The trade for provisions I directed to be carried on at the tent by Mr. Peckover.*

Fletcher Christian was put in charge of the breadfruit plants and spent most of the time ashore. By then the men aboard the ships that had called at the island had spread venereal diseases among the natives. Eighteen of the *Bounty*'s crew, including Christian, contracted venereal diseases while in Tahiti.

When the time came to leave, inevitably there were tensions as the crew had to be brought back to a state of efficiency for the voyage home. Later, stories were told of disputes between Bligh and Christian but most of them were of a trivial nature.

Stacked coconuts at a coconut stall, Mysore city market, India. Photo by Kelsi Nagy, 2010

The most famous story was the affair of the coconuts. Bligh obtained a supply of coconuts in Tahiti and said he had intended to keep them for later in the voyage, as the ship would be many weeks at sea and the crew would be glad of fresh provisions. Coconuts were especially valuable as they provided food and drink in a form that could be stored.

The coconuts kept disappearing, however, and, being unable to discover the culprits, Bligh had the rest distributed among the crew so that everyone would get their fair share.

John Fryer, the Master, said that Bligh accused:

> *all the young gentlemen and people*

of stealing the coconuts but Edward Christian alleged that Bligh accused Fletcher Christian, saying:

> *Damn your blood, you have stolen my cocoa nuts.*

and that Christian replied:

> *I was dry, I thought it of no consequence, I took one only.*

Whatever the details, it was obviously a petty quarrel but Christian later told the carpenter, William Purcell, that he was afraid Bligh would:

> *break me, turn me before the mast, and perhaps flog me; and if he did, it would be the death of us both, for I am sure I should take him in my arms, and jump overboard with him.*

It is clear that Bligh never had any intention of doing any of these things. In fact, he invited Christian to supper that night but Christian said he was too ill to go.

There have been various attempts to rationalise Fletcher Christian's conduct by arguing on the one hand, that he was desperate to return to his girl in Tahiti, or on the other, that he was driven to desperation by Bligh's swearing and quarrels about coconuts and the like. Christian's defenders claim that he felt so insulted at being accused of stealing coconuts that he stole the ship and put the lives of all the crew in danger, facing them, as Heywood said:

> *with a Choice of Deaths.*

Fletcher Christian's action was as irrational as a crew member hijacking an aeroplane and claiming it was because the captain had accused him of stealing the duty-free drinks. His change of attitude was so violent and his actions so aberrant for a naval officer that they suggest he was suffering from paranoid delusions. Thomas Ellison, one of the mutineers, said he:

> *looked like a madman.*

Bligh believed Christian was insane.

Captain Bligh in Wapping 1785–1790

A contemporary impression by an unknown artist of Fletcher Christian at the time of the mutiny

This theory has been strengthened by a revelation that Christian's brother, Charles, was involved in a mutiny in September 1787, while surgeon of a merchant ship, the *Middlesex*.

Freud said that paranoid delusions arose from repressed homosexuality. By repressed he meant emotions that were regarded as so shameful that they were not admitted to the conscious mind but were banished to the subconscious where they were distorted into delusions of persecution. The Georgian Navy was conducive to such mental illness because the Articles of War laid down the death penalty for:

> *the unnatural and detestable Sin of Buggery or Sodomy with Man or Beast.*

Maurice Bligh, Captain Bligh's great-great-great-grandson, has suggested that Fletcher Christian displayed symptoms of suffering from narcotics withdrawal:

> Medical encyclopaedias list opioid withdrawal reactions in progressive stages over a period of twelve to thirty hours. These include agitation and anxiety, muscle aches, sleeplessness and yawning, a runny nose, abdominal cramps, diarrhoea, nausea, vomiting, dilated pupils and abnormal sweating.
>
> Christian was observed as having an unkempt appearance and "horrible" countenance. His face was gaunt from a loss of appetite and insomnia. His behaviour was erratic. He had "wild eyes" and sweated profusely from the face and hands "so that he soils everything he handles". Notably none of these physical manifestations were ever reported about him in previous years when he sailed with Captain Bligh.

4 - Tahiti

> When pirating the *Bounty*, Christian became a man "who didn't know whether to throw himself or everyone else overboard". But within hours after the ship was taken and access to a supply of laudanum (a tincture of raw opium and alcohol) was established, he became subdued, shutting himself in his cabin, head in hands, speaking to no-one for days.

The *Bounty*'s surgeon, Thomas Huggan, was an alcoholic. He would have had a supply of laudanum and could have been trading it with Christian for rum but Huggan died in Tahiti and was replaced by Thomas Denman Ledward.

Ledward wrote a letter home, in which he said:

> *as soon as I was informed fully how the matter stood I instantly declared I would go with the captain, let the consequences be what it would, and not stay among mutineers.*

He also wrote that he was deprived of:

> *every individual thing I took out with me, beside effects to a considerable amount which I purchased at the Surgeon, Mr Huggan's death.*

The laudanum was, therefore, left in the ship.

Medicine chest belonging to Sir Benjamin F Outram KCB (1774–1856) and reputedly used at the Battle of Copenhagen, 1801. Photo by John Tarby, 2017

Captain Bligh in Wapping 1785–1790

It is possible that Fletcher Christian was addicted to laudanum.

Whether he took it to relieve his paranoia, or whether the paranoia arose from the addiction, it is impossible to judge but paranoics can persuade groups of people or even whole nations to follow them and share their delusions, usually leading them to disaster.

When the legend of Bligh as a tyrannical flogging captain is compared with the reality that he was one of the least severe of 18th-century sea captains, it is clear that the legend is a product of Christian's paranoid delusions. Christian did not, in fact, accuse Bligh of ill-treating the crew but only of ill-treating him, saying:

Why do you use me thus, Captain Bligh?

Laudanum
A tincture of opium containing approximately 10% powdered opium. Reddish-brown and extremely bitter, laudanum contains almost all of the opium alkaloids, including morphine and codeine, and its high morphine concentration makes it a potent narcotic. Today, laudanum is recognised as addictive and is strictly regulated.

5 - Mutiny

The volcano eruption on Tofua prior to the mutiny, as depicted on a 1953 Tongan postage stamp

On the night of 28th April 1789, Peckover's watch took over from Fryer's as usual. Most of the crew were on deck, watching a volcano erupt on the nearby island of Tofua in the South Pacific ocean. The excitement died down and Peckover's watch was uneventful. It was a fine, calm night.

In the early hours of the next morning, Peckover's watch was relieved by Christian's and Peckover went to bed. He had only just fallen asleep when, he said:

> *I was awaked from my sleep by a confused noise, and directly afterwards thought I heard the fixing of bayonets: I jumped up, and at the door met Mr. Nelson; he told me the ship was taken from us.*

Possibly with Captain Cook's fate on his mind, Peckover thought that they had been boarded by hostile natives and protested:

> *We were a long way from land, when I came off deck.*

Nelson replied:

> *It is by our own people, Christian at their head.*

The trust that Bligh had put in Christian placed him in a position where he was able to seize the ship, even though more than half the crew remained loyal to Bligh. As officer of the watch, Christian "had the ship" and access to the Captain's cabin, as Bligh said:

> *I slept with the door always open, that the officer of the watch might have access to me on all occasions. The possibility of such a conspiracy was ever the farthest from my thoughts.*

Fletcher Christian was also able to obtain the key to the arms chest and to arm his followers before he and three others went to Bligh's cabin and took him prisoner.

Bligh was taken completely by surprise, as were the loyal officers. Heywood wrote of:

> *every person being as it were infatuated, and not knowing what to do.*

Peckover suggested:

> *Let us go forward and see what's to be done.*

But, he said:

> *On going to the hatchway to get up, we were stopped by Sumner and Quintal, by a fixed bayonet down the hatchway, who said, "Peckover you can't come up: we have mutinied, and taken the ship."*

Peckover continued:

> *In a short while, Mr, Samuel came down, and said he was going away in the small cutter with Captain Bligh…*

5 - Mutiny

> *... He advised with me what he should take with him, I advised him but a few things, he took only a few shirts and stockings in a bag. Mr. Fryer came down afterwards, and asked me what I meant to do; I told him I wished to do for the best, and to get home if I could.*

Fryer suggested a different plan:

> *If you are ordered into the boat, say you will stay on board: and I flatter myself we shall restore the ship in a short time.*

Peckover objected:

> *If we stay, we shall all be deemed pirates.*

Fryer assured him that he had the Captain's consent to his plan but the mutineers became suspicious and ordered them on deck. They found that the Captain was to have the launch, a larger boat, instead of the cutter.

The full-size replica of Bounty's launch built by the National Maritime Museum, Cornwall and displayed in their "Capt. Bligh: Myth, Man & Mutiny" exhibition. Photo by John Tarby, 2017

Captain Bligh in Wapping 1785–1790

Peckover said:

> *I came naked on the quarter deck, except my trowsers.*

and:

> *I saw Captain Bligh and Christian alongside of him with a naked bayonet, I asked Christian to let me go down forward, to get my things out of my chest: Christian said, "You have no things down aft," I said "Only a few" then stept to the gangway, and went over the side.*

Peckover wrote:

> *Coleman called to me over the stern, and begged I would call on his friend at Greenwich and acquaint him of the matter. I think he said he wished to come into the boat.*

But there was no room – the launch was already overladen.

Joseph Coleman was the armourer. He and three others, Charles Norman, Thomas McIntosh and Michael Byrne, were kept in the ship against their will. They were all exonerated in Bligh's log.

Had he really been as harsh as depicted, Bligh would probably have been murdered by the mutineers, who were soon drunk and armed with muskets.

Examples of late 18th-century flintlock sea service muskets

Sea musket

As early as 1738, Britain's Admiralty had muskets made specifically for its sailors and marines. The muskets were produced in both a bright finish and a blackened or japanned finish. It was said that seamen's time was better spent in seafaring than polishing, so blackening the barrels of their muskets to protect them from salty sea water was the better option.

5 - Mutiny

"Mutiny on the Bounty" by Robert Dodd, 1790

Peter Heywood did not go into the boat. He said:

> *to be starved to death, or drowned, appeared to be inevitable if I went in the boat.*

One of those kept in the ship against their will, Charles Norman, the carpenter's mate, had a wife and children in England. Midshipman John Hallett, who was in the boat, said:

> *just before we came away he was crying and saying that he wished he could go with us to see his Wife and Family.*

Norman protested to Christian afterwards:

> *This is a hard case upon me, Mr Christian, who have a wife and family in England.*

Captain Bligh in Wapping 1785–1790

According to Edward Christian, his brother replied:

It is a hard case, Norman, but it never would have happened if I could have left the ship alone.

Bligh was unable to account for Christian's actions and said:

Consider Mr Christian, I have a wife and four children in England, and you have danced my children upon your knee.

According to his brother:

Christian afterwards told the people in the ship, that when Bligh spoke of his wife and children, my heart melted, and I would then have jumped overboard, if I could have saved you.

and Christian declared that:

he would readily sacrifice his own life, if the persons in the launch were all safe in the ship again.

1989 postage stamp depicting Bligh and the crew cast adrift

6 - Voyage Home

Life-sized replica of the Bounty's launch showing interior. Photo by John Tarby, 2017

Bligh examined the provisions in the launch and found they had food and water for five days. The nearest port was Coupang (now Kupang) in Timor, over four thousand miles away, a voyage of at least six weeks. Peckover had made the voyage with Cook in the *Endeavour* and was able to provide useful information. Bligh also recorded that Peckover had brought his watch with him, so that they were able to regulate their time, until it stopped on 2nd June.

Examples of typical late 18th-century pocket watches

The K2 chronometer assigned to William Bligh for the voyage

Bounty's chronometer
After the mutiny, the K2 chronometer (a copy of Harrison's H4 and which is 5" diameter) remained with the mutineers on Pitcairn until Captain Matthew Folger of the American whaling ship *Topaz of Boston* discovered the women, children and the surviving mutineer, John Adams, in 1808. Folger purchased the chronometer from John Adams. Adams received a "small silk handkerchief he prized" for the chronometer and the *Bounty's* azimuth compass.

Captain Bligh in Wapping 1785–1790

Bligh and the 18 men with him landed on the nearby island of Tofua to obtain provisions but the natives attacked them, killing one man, John Norton. After that they decided to make the food last, although it meant living on an ounce of bread and a quarter of a pint of water a day.

Route of the 4,000 mile voyage taken by Bligh after the mutiny—from near Tofua in the east to Timor in the west

The launch met with rough seas and violent storms and as a result the men were constantly wet and exhausted from baling the water out of the boat but they arrived safely in Timor on 14th June 1789 and Bligh wrote:

> *Our bodies were nothing but skin and bones, our limbs were full of sores, and we were cloathed in rags; in this condition, with the tears of joy and gratitude flowing down our cheeks, the people of Timor beheld us with a mixture of horror, surprise and pity.*

As soon as he could, Bligh wrote to his wife:

> *What an emotion does my heart & soul feel that I have once more an opportunity of writing to you and my little Angels, and particularly as you have all been so near losing the best of friends…*

6 - Voyage Home

William Bligh and his crew received by the Governor of Timor, 14th June 1789

> *... when you would have had no person to have regarded you as I do, and you must have spent the remainder of your days without knowing what was become of me, or what would have been still worse, to have known I had been starved to Death at Sea or destroyed by Indians... Know then my own Dear Betsy, I have lost the Bounty.*

He concluded:

> *Give my blessing to my dear Harriet, my dear Mary, my dear Betsy and to my dear little stranger and tell them I shall soon be home.*

The climate of the East Indies was unhealthy and in their weakened condition five of Bligh's men died of fevers. The first to die was David Nelson, the botanist. Bligh was particularly affected by his death and wrote in his Log:

> *The Mango Trees are now in blossom and some of the Jambolang, and the Bushes in general indicate the advance of Spring. All these circumstances recall to me the loss of Mr Nelson and the object of my Voyage, which at times almost bear me down, but for the impropriety to let so much Weakness get the better of me.*

Captain Bligh in Wapping 1785–1790

Bligh was himself seized with a "violent fever". He recovered but said:

> *for a long time I continued very weak and infirm.*

He sailed for Europe on 2nd January 1790, arriving back in England on the 14th March to find his family had increased by not one but two little strangers, twin girls, Frances and Jane.

When Bligh returned to Wapping, he received a letter from Charles Norman's brother-in-law, who was taking care of Norman's wife, Ann, and their children.

Bligh replied:

No 4 Broad Street St George's East

March 26th 1790

Sir

Your unfortunate Brother, Charles Norman, was Carpenters Mate with me & was kept in the Ship against his will, and I have recommended him to Mercy – his friends may therefore be easy in their minds on his account as it is most likely he will return by the first Ship that comes from Otaheite... He was in very good health.

I am Your Humble Serv.

Wm Bligh

I only rec.d your letter today.

6 - Voyage Home

The Royalty Theatre on Well Street

In May 1790, the first dramatic version of the mutiny, *The Pirates*, was put on at the Royalty Theatre in Well Street (now Ensign Street), on the north side of Ratcliffe Highway (now The Highway). Bligh was played by Ralph Wewitzer, the actor-manager, and Fletcher Christian by William Bourke, who was expert at dancing the hornpipe.

The Royalty was famous for special effects and nautical subjects. The death of Captain Cook was also staged there and, later, the Battle of Trafalgar and the death of Nelson.

Ralph Wewitzer, comedian and actor-manager of the Royalty Theatre, by J S Agar, 1806

A view of a stage set at the Royalty Theatre

A view of the auditorium at the Royalty Theatre

6 - Voyage Home

ROYALTY-THEATRE,
Well-Street, near Goodman's-Fields.

This present THURSDAY, May 6, 1790,
WILL BE PRESENTED
A NEW MUSICAL PIECE, called

TAR against PERFUME:
Or, The SAILOR PREFERRED.

Coxswain, Mr. MATHEWS. William, Mr. BIRKETT. Old Slop, Mr. REES. And Monsieur Le Friz, (the Perfumer,) Mr. WEWITZER.
Susan, Miss WILLIAMS.
A NEW DANCE, composed by Mr. BOURKE, called

THE MERRY BLOCK-MAKERS.

By Monf. FERRERE, Mad. FOUZZI, Mad. FERRERE, Mr. JEANI, Mr. BOURKE, &c.
A MUSICAL ENTERTAINMENT, called

A PILL FOR THE DOCTOR:
Or, The TRIPLE WEDDING.

Sailor, Mr. BIRKETT. Dr. Lotion, Mr. REES. Farmer, Mr. MATHEWS. And Pestle, the Doctor's Man, Mr. WEWITZER.
Polly, Miss WILLIAMS   Dorothy, Mrs. SAUNDERS.
Lydia, Miss E. WILLIAMS.   And Goody, Mrs. BURNETT.
To conclude with a DANCE by the Characters.
A FAVOURITE SONG, by Miss DANIEL.
The Whole to conclude with (the 4th Time) A FACT, TOLD IN ACTION, called

The PIRATES:
OR,
The Calamities of Capt. BLIGH.

Exhibiting a full Account of his Voyage, from his taking Leave at the Admiralty.
AND SHEWING,
The BOUNTY falling down the River THAMES.
The Captain's Reception at OTAHEITE, and exchanging the *British Manufactures* for the BREAD-FRUIT TREES. With an OTAHEITEAN DANCE.
The Attachment of the OTAHEITEAN WOMEN to, and then Distress at parting from, the BRITISH SAILORS.
An exact Representation of
The SEISURE of Capt. BLIGH, in the Cabin of the BOUNTY, by the Pirates.
With the affecting Scene of forcing the Captain and his faithful Followers into the Boat.
Their Distress at Sea, and Repulse by the Natives of One of the *Friendly Islands*.
Their miraculous Arrival at the *Cape of Good Hope*, and their friendly Reception by the Governor.
DANCES and CEREMONIES of the HOTTENTOTS
On their Departure. And their happy Arrival in England.
Rehearsed under the immediate Instruction of a Person who was on-board the Bounty, Store-Ship.
*** The Doors to be opened at Half past Five and to begin at Half past Six o'Clock precisely.
BOXES, 3s. 6d.—PIT, 2s. 6d.—FIRST GALLERY, 1s. 6d.—UPPER GALLERY, 1s.
Nothing under full Price will be taken nor any Money returned:
Places for the Boxes may be taken at the Stage-Door from Ten till Three o'Clock every Day.
VIVANT REX & REGINA.
☞ BOOKS of the PILL for the DOCTOR to be had at the Theatre; and, to prevent Imposition, the Proprietors have ordered that no more shall be taken for them than SIX-PENCE each.

The playbill for the dramatised version of the mutiny, "The Pirates or The Calamities of Capt. Bligh", 1790

A playbill seller outside the Royalty Theatre

Captain Bligh in Wapping 1785–1790

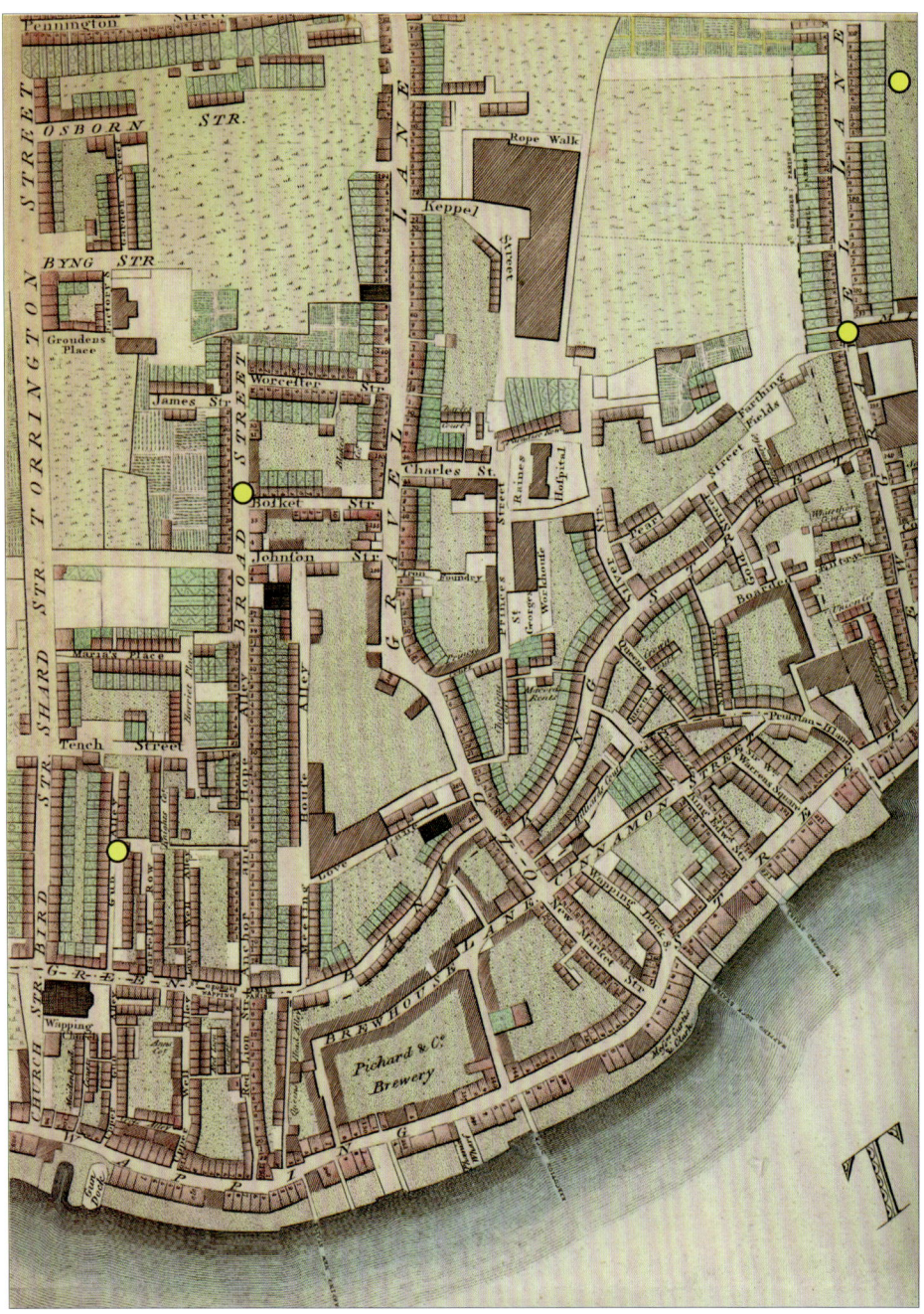

Disposition of the HM Ship Providence's crew who lived in Wapping and Shadwell (homes shown in yellow)

7 - Breadfruit Success

Later in 1790, Bligh and his family moved from Wapping to No 14 North Moor Place, Lambeth, south London, probably because his house was threatened with demolition to make way for the building of the London Docks. He was court-martialled for the loss of his ship but was exonerated and promoted to post captain, that is captain by rank.

In 1791 Bligh was given command of HM Ship *Providence* and sent again to transplant the breadfruit tree from Tahiti to the West Indies.

Although Bligh was no longer living in Wapping, the area was not unrepresented on his new ship. Five seamen were recruited in the Roundhouse, a public house in New Gravel Lane (now Garnet Street) and the surgeon's mate, Robert Ridgeway, came from Shadwell. It is possible that the second lieutenant, James Guthrie, lived in Wapping as the land tax records show a James Guthrie living in Broad Street (now Reardon Street).

Peckover, who had returned safely to Gun Alley, applied to be gunner of the *Providence* but Bligh decided not to take any of the *Bounty*'s officers. Peckover was then about 45 years old and suffered from rheumatism, so was probably not fit enough for such a strenuous voyage.

Bligh sailed past Wapping in the *Providence* as he set sail on his second breadfruit voyage in 1791.

He took two seamen from the *Bounty*, Lawrence Lebogue and John Smith but the voyage proved too much for Smith and Bligh had to send him home from the Cape of Good Hope.

A year earlier, Captain Edward Edwards had been sent in HM Ship *Pandora* to search for the mutineers. He found 14 of the *Bounty*'s crew, including Peter Heywood and Charles Norman, in Tahiti and took them prisoner.

The water-stained page of Bligh's log documenting the crew members of the Bounty and their status in the mutiny

Captain Bligh in Wapping 1785–1790

HM Ship Pandora sinking in 1791, from a sketch by Peter Heywood

The *Pandora* was wrecked on the return voyage but Heywood and Norman survived and reached England. Heywood wrote to Mrs Bligh from HMS *Hector* protesting his innocence, and saying:

> *I have one request to ask of you, Madam, which is, that you will be so obliging as to inquire whether Mrs Duncan, in Little Hermitage-street, hath in her possession the clothes (which, if you remember) I left with her in 1787.*

Bligh was not at the court martial of the mutineers in 1792 as he had already set out on his second breadfruit voyage but Norman produced Bligh's letter and was acquitted, with the others exonerated by Bligh. Heywood said of Bligh:

> *from his attention to and very kind treatment of me personally, I should have been a monster of depravity to have betrayed him.*

Heywood was found guilty but recommended to mercy and pardoned. He then joined with Edward Christian in his attack on Bligh's character, describing Fletcher Christian as:

> *beloved by all (except one, whose ill report is his greatest praise).*

7 - Breadfruit Success

Isle of Man stamp issued in 1989 showing Fletcher Christian at home on Pitcairn Island. The portrait is by an unknown 19th-century artist and is not drawn from life but from description

Fletcher Christian and eight of the mutineers eventually settled on Pitcairn Island in the southern Pacific Ocean. When the settlement was discovered in 1808, there was only one mutineer left alive, John Adams.

John Adams on Pitcairn Island, sketched in 1829

John Adams wrote an account of the mutiny, in which he declared that:

> *there was no real discontent among the crew; much less was there any idea of offering violence to their commander.*

but that they were persuaded to mutiny as:

> *success would restore them all to the happy island, and the connections they had left behind.*

Captain Bligh in Wapping 1785-1790

Adams had a brother, Jonathan, who lived in Wapping in Upper Gun Alley (now close to St Patrick's church). Jonathan had been aboard the *Bounty* as a boy of 13 to say farewell when John had joined the ship at Deptford, south-east London.

"Deptford Dockyard" by F Smith, 1779

A gentleman named Thomas Walters wrote to the *Gentleman's Magazine* on 4th November 1818:

> *Having been informed that John Adams, the last survivor of the Bounty's crew on the island had a brother, I desired to see him: he called on me, is a waterman at Union Stairs, wears the fire coat of the London Assurance, and is, of course, a steady character.*

On hearing of the discovery of his brother on Pitcairn:

> *he was much affected; said he accompanied him on board the Bounty at Deptford.*

Jonathan wrote a letter to his brother, which was delivered by Captain Henderson of the *Hercules*, who wrote:

7 - Breadfruit Success

> *I delivered to Adams the box of Books from the Missionary Society of London, and a Letter from Adams' brother, who is still living at Wapping in London. I read this Letter to him, giving him a description of his family, mentioning the death of one sister, and the prosperity of another. This affected him much, and he often repeated that he never expected to see this day.*

Remnants of Union Stairs and causeway at Wapping. Photo by John Tarby, 2014

Alan Adams, a descendant of Jonathan Adams, has carried out extensive research into his family history. It shows that Jonathan later worked from Wapping New Stairs, near the Thames River Police station in Wapping High Street.

Upper Gun Alley was in the parish of St John of Wapping and Jonathan's first son, Andrew Steadman Adams, was baptised in St John's in 1797.

Jonathan later moved to Knight's Court, where the John Orwell Sports Centre is now, and lived there until his death in 1842. Knight's Court was in the parish of St George-in-the-East and children born there were baptised in St George's. These included Jonathan's second son, John Adams (Alan's ancestor), who was baptised in 1803.

Detail from Richard Horwood's Plan of London (1799), showing the location of Gun Alley

John Adams joined the Thames River Police in 1826. He was then living in Old Gravel Lane (now Wapping Lane). He continued to serve in what later became known as the Thames Division of the Metropolitan Police until 1856 and his family remained in Wapping until later in the century.

7 - Breadfruit Success

"Transplanting of the Bread Fruit Trees from Otaheite" by Thomas Gosse, 1796

The *Providence* succeeded where the *Bounty* had failed and Bligh delivered the breadfruit to the West Indies in 1793. It is still grown and eaten there and is now imported into Great Britain and sold in various outlets, among them Deptford Market.

The houses on the west side of Broad Street were compulsorily purchased and demolished by the London Dock Company under powers given to them by the London Dock Act 1800. The dock wall was built along that side of the street.

In 1941, St George-in-the-East, a Nicholas Hawksmoor church, was hit by a German incendiary bomb and the interior was gutted. The building was

Breadfruit on sale in a shop in Deptford, south London. Photo by John Tarby, 2017

Captain Bligh in Wapping 1785–1790

The site of Peckover's house at 13 Gun Alley, now in Wapping Gardens. Photo by John Tarby, 2017

Blue plaque on London Docks wall in Reardon Street at the site of Bligh's house in Wapping. Photo by John Tarby, 2017

7 - Breadfruit Success

restored after the war as a smaller church constructed inside the original walls.

The site of Peckover's house is now inside Wapping Gardens, also known as Wapping Park. The street where Bligh lived is now called Reardon Street.

The docks closed in 1969 but the dock wall remains, with a plaque marking the site where Bligh lived with his family, where Fletcher Christian visited him and danced his little girls on his knee, and where Heywood stayed and sent his washing to Mrs Duncan in the Hermitage, before they set sail on their fateful voyage in the *Bounty*.

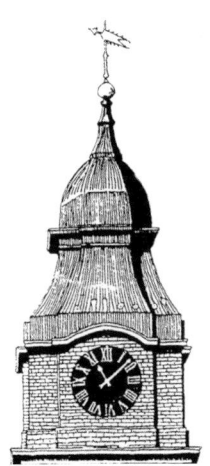

Captain Bligh in Wapping 1785–1790

About the Author

Madge Darby was born in Old Gravel Lane, now Wapping Lane, in 1927, just five minutes' walk from where she lives today. Resident at Pier Head in Wapping High Street since 1975, Madge has lived in Wapping all her life.

The Darby family history stretches back many generations. The earliest written ancestry is the baptism of Elizabeth Darby in 1636 which can be found in the 17th-century registers of St John of Wapping. On her mother's side, Madge Darby's great-great-grandfather, Robert Petley, and his family, lived at 25 St Katharine's Square in the Precinct of St Katharine. They were among the people turned out of their homes when the docks were built at the beginning of the 19th century.

Educated at Raine's School in Arbour Square, Stepney and then in Dalston before taking a BA (Hons) degree in History at Queen Mary College, University of London, Madge has been a prolific writer and editor on people and events that have involved the area. Topics have included the history of Wapping and St Katharine's, William Peckover, Judge Jeffreys, the Hermitage Shelter, Tender Grace (a collection of letters and diaries telling the intertwining histories of her family and Wapping from 1886–2000) and Captain Bligh.

Bligh and his family were living in Wapping when he was appointed to command the *Bounty* and set out on his famous voyage. Madge's latest book gives new insight into the connections with Wapping of William Bligh and some of the *Bounty's* crew and is published to coincide with the 200th anniversary of Bligh's death on 7th December 1817.

About the Trust
The History of Wapping Trust was set up in 1984 to promote the history of the area by talks, walks, publications, Christmas cards and postcards. We work closely with other Wapping groups by providing historical information.

Additional Information

Bibliography

Sources:

The National Archives, Kew (formerly the Public Record Office)

Log of the Bounty 1787–1789 (ADM 55/151)

[This is Bligh's official Log. It is a fair copy made for the Admiralty by the ship's clerk, John Samuel, and is signed by Bligh.]

Bligh's Court Martial for the loss of the ship, 22 October 1790 (ADM1/5328)

Court Martial of the Bounty Mutineers, 12–18 September 1792 (ADM1/5330 Part 2)

[The accused were Midshipmen Peter Heywood, James Morrison, Charles Norman, Thomas McIntosh, Joseph Coleman, William Muspratt, Thomas Burkett, John Millward, Thomas Ellison and Michael Byrne.

They were charged with "mutinously running away with His Majesty's Armed Vessel Bounty and deserting from His Majesty's Service."

Norman, McIntosh, Coleman and Byrne were acquitted.

Heywood, Morrison and Muspratt were pardoned.

Burkett, Millward and Ellison were hanged].

London Metropolitan Archives (formerly the Greater London Record Office)

Parish Registers of St George-in-the-East, Baptismal Register 1777–94 (P93/GEO/4)

Guildhall Library, London

Land Tax Record, Lower St George's, Part 11, page 60, 1785–1789 (6016 91-99)

Plymouth and West Devon Record Office, Plymouth

The Minster Church of St Andrew, Plymouth

Published works:

ADAMS, Alan. Divided by the Bounty, 2010.

BARNEY, Stephen. Minutes of the Proceedings of the Court Martial on Ten Persons charged with Mutiny on Board His Majesty's Ship the BOUNTY, 1794. Contains an Appendix by Edward Christian.

[Barney was the counsel for Muspratt. His account differs in places from the official Minutes and contains only the evidence for the Prosecution. This is probably because none of the defendants pleaded ill-treatment by Bligh in mitigation and some claimed that Fletcher Christian had forced them to join the mutiny. Ellison said that Fletcher Christian looked like a madman and kept everyone in fear of him.]

BLIGH, William. A Narrative of the Mutiny on board His Majesty's Ship Bounty and the subsequent voyage of part of the crew in the ship's boat, from Tofoa, one of the Friendly Islands, to Timor, a Dutch settlement in the East Indies, 1790.

BLIGH, William. A Voyage to the South Sea Undertaken by Command of His Majesty for the Purpose of Conveying the Bread-Fruit Tree to the West Indies in His Majesty's Ship the Bounty, Commanded by Lieutenant William Bligh and an Account of The Mutiny on Board HMS Bounty and the Subsequent Voyage of Part of the Crew, in the Ship's Boat from Tofoa, one of the Friendly Islands, to Timor, a Dutch Settlement in the East Indies, 1792.

[The Narrative was produced quickly, in response to public demand, and contains only the mutiny and open boat voyage. The Voyage was produced later and contains the whole voyage.]

BLIGH, William. An Answer to Certain Assertions, 1794.

[This is Bligh's answer to Edward Christian's Appendix.]

DARBY, Madge. Who Caused the Mutiny on the Bounty?, 1965.

DENING, Greg. Mr Bligh's Bad Language: Passion, Power and Theatre on The Bounty, 1992.

KENNEDY, Gavin. Bligh, 1978.

KENNEDY, Gavin. Captain Bligh: The Man and His Mutinies, 1989.

MACKANESS, George. The Life of Vice-Admiral William Bligh R.N., F.R.S., 1951.

SPENCE, Jack. Plymouth Minster: A History of St Andrew's, 2011.

Captain Bligh in Wapping 1785-1790

Other History of Wapping Trust Publications

- *Waeppa's People – A History of Wapping* by Madge Darby,
  A5, softback, 90pp, illustrated, £3.50 (out of print)
  Pub. 1988 by Conner & Butler, ISBN 0 947699

- *William Peckover of Wapping – Gunner of the Bounty* by Madge Darby, A5, softback, illustrated, maps 14pp, £1.00
  Pub. 1989 by Conner & Butler, ISBN 0 947699 12 0

- *Judge Jeffreys and the Ivy Case* by Madge Darby,
  A5, softback, illustrated, maps, 42pp, £3.00
  Pub. 1989 by Conner & Butler, ISBN 0 947699 13 9

- *Captain Bligh in Wapping* by Madge Darby,
  A5, softback, 18pp, illustrated, map, £1.20 (out of print)
  Pub. 1990 History of Wapping Trust, ISBN 1 873086 00 8

- *Colonel Thomas Rainsborough – Wapping's Most Famous Soldier (1610-1648)* by Lincoln S Jones,
  A5, softback, illustrated, map, 18pp, £1.20
  Pub. 1990 by History of Wapping Trust, ISBN 1 873086 03 2

- *The Hermitage Shelter Minutes – December 1940* (An air-raid shelter in Hermitage Wharf) edited by Madge Darby,
  A5, softback, illustrated, map, 18pp, £1.20
  Pub. 1990 by History of Wapping Trust, ISBN 1 873086 01 6

- *A Riverside Journey in Picture Postcards – from Tower Bridge to Blackwall Pier* by Steve Kentfield, Ray Newton,
  A4, softback, 54pp, £4.95
  Pub. 1990 by History of Wapping Trust, ISBN 1 873086 02 4

- *South of Commercial Road – A Photographic Record 1934-1997* by Ray Newton, John Tarby, Steve Kentfield, Tom Newton,
  A4, softback, 44pp, £5.95
  Pub. 2001 by History of Wapping Trust, ISBN 1 873086 04 0

- *Piety and Piracy – The History of Wapping and St Katharine's* by Madge Darby,
  Royal Octavo perfect bound, 96pp, £9.95
  Pub. 2011 by History of Wapping Trust, ISBN 978-1 873086 06 3